Welcome to the wonderful world of kawaii! This coloring book is filled with adorable and charming illustrations that will bring a smile to your face. From cute animals to yummy treats, these full-page drawings are just waiting for you to add your own personal touch. Kawaii, which means "cute" in Japanese, is a style that is loved all around the world. It's known for its bright colors, round shapes, and sweet expressions. In this coloring book, you'll find plenty of kawaii characters to color in, from unicorns to pandas. Whether you're a fan of coloring or just love cute things, this book is sure to provide hours of entertainment. So grab your favorite coloring tools and let your imagination run wild as you bring these adorable kawaii illustrations to life!

Roxhanzo

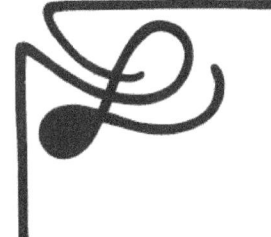
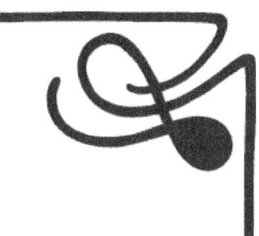

THIS BOOK
BELONGS TO:

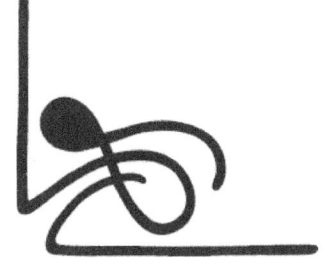
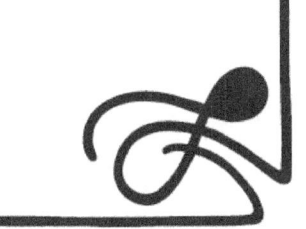

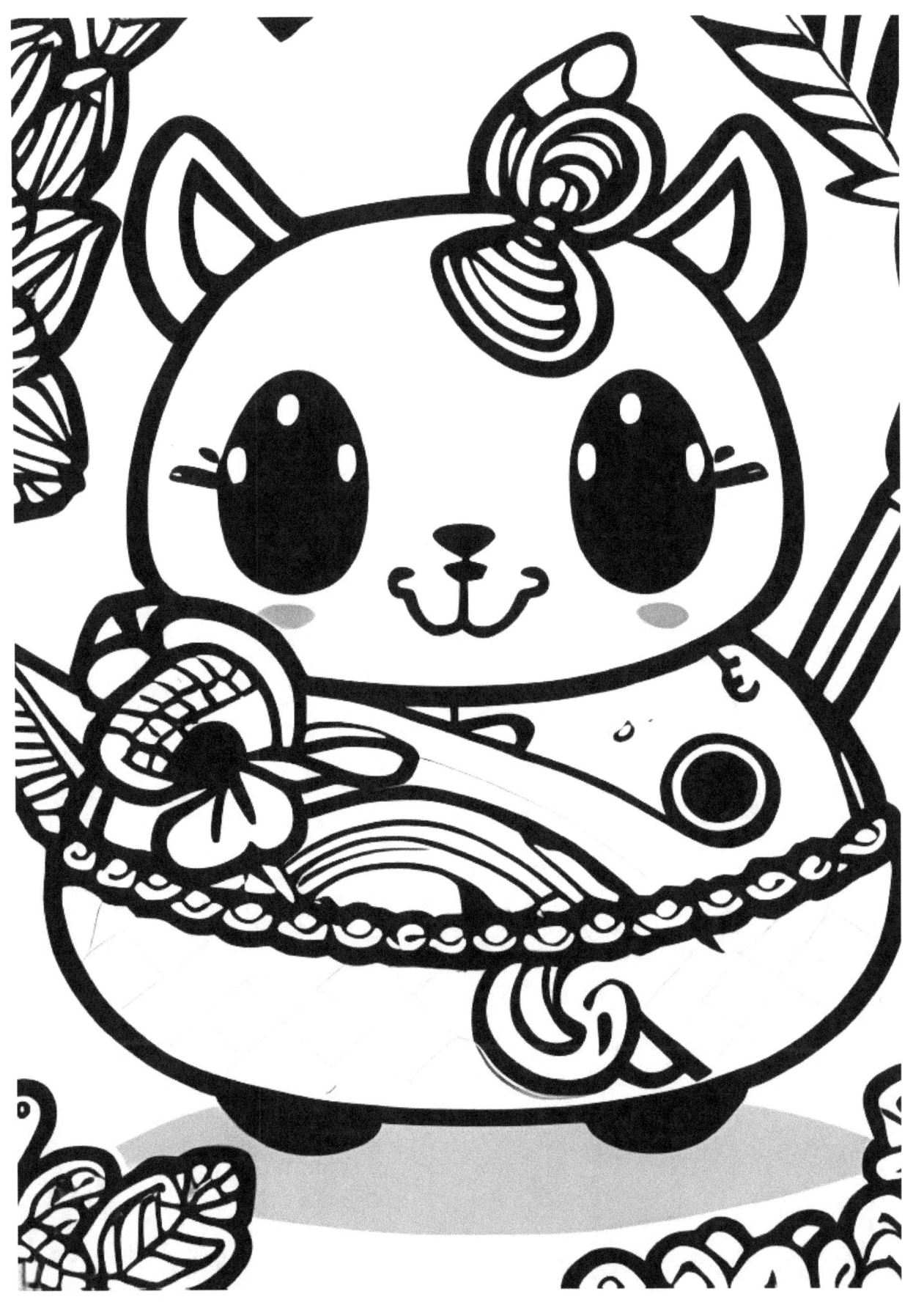

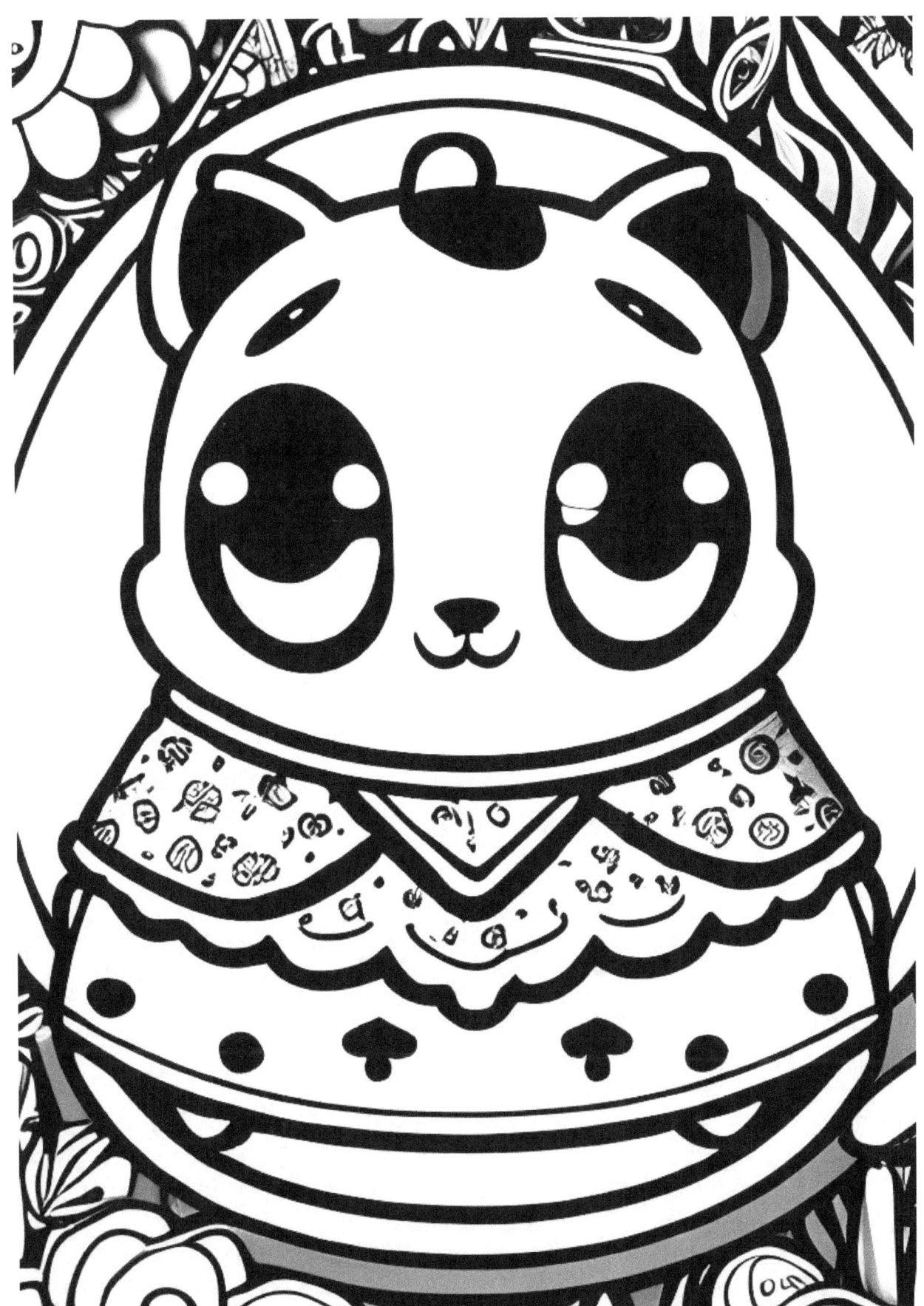

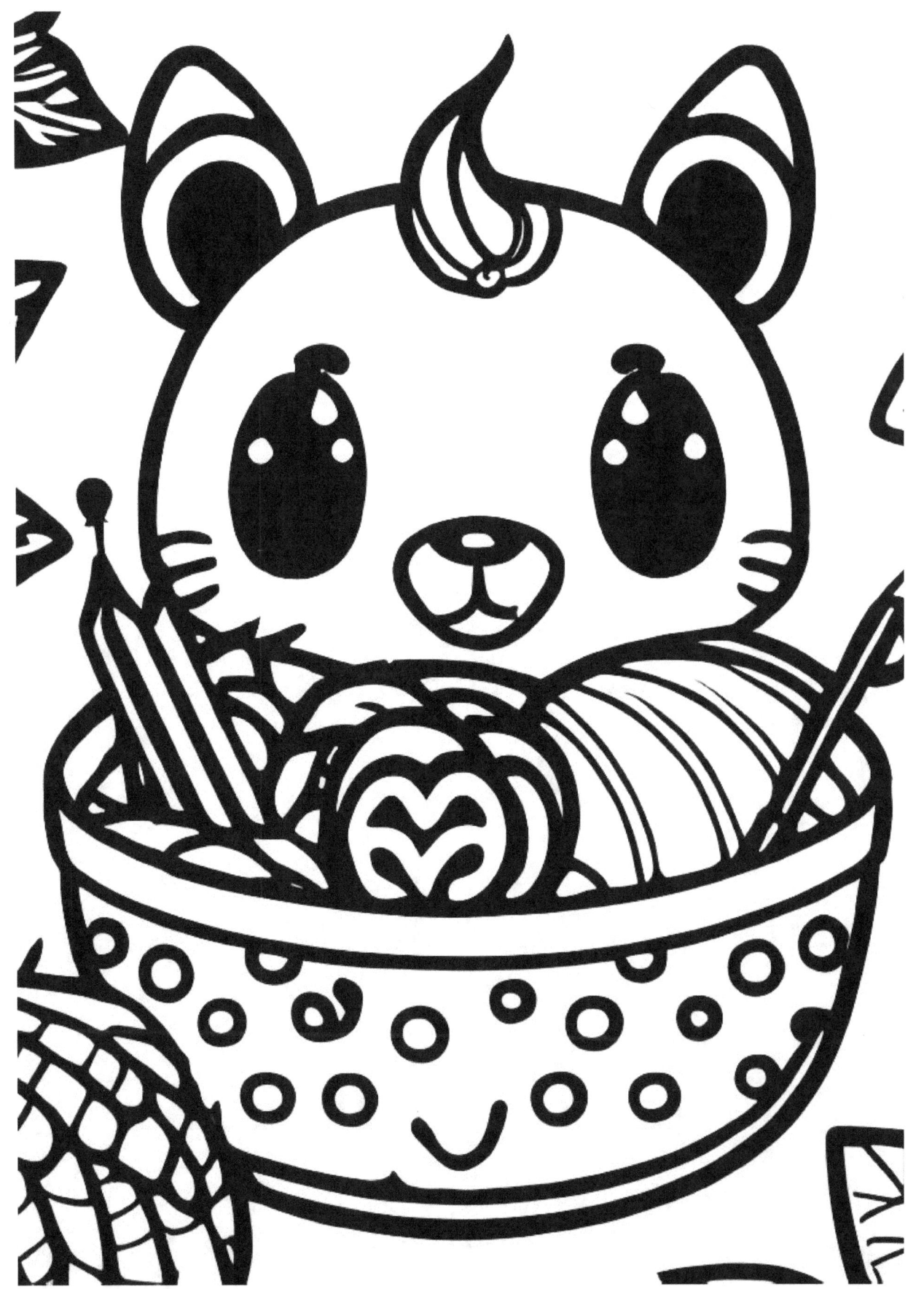

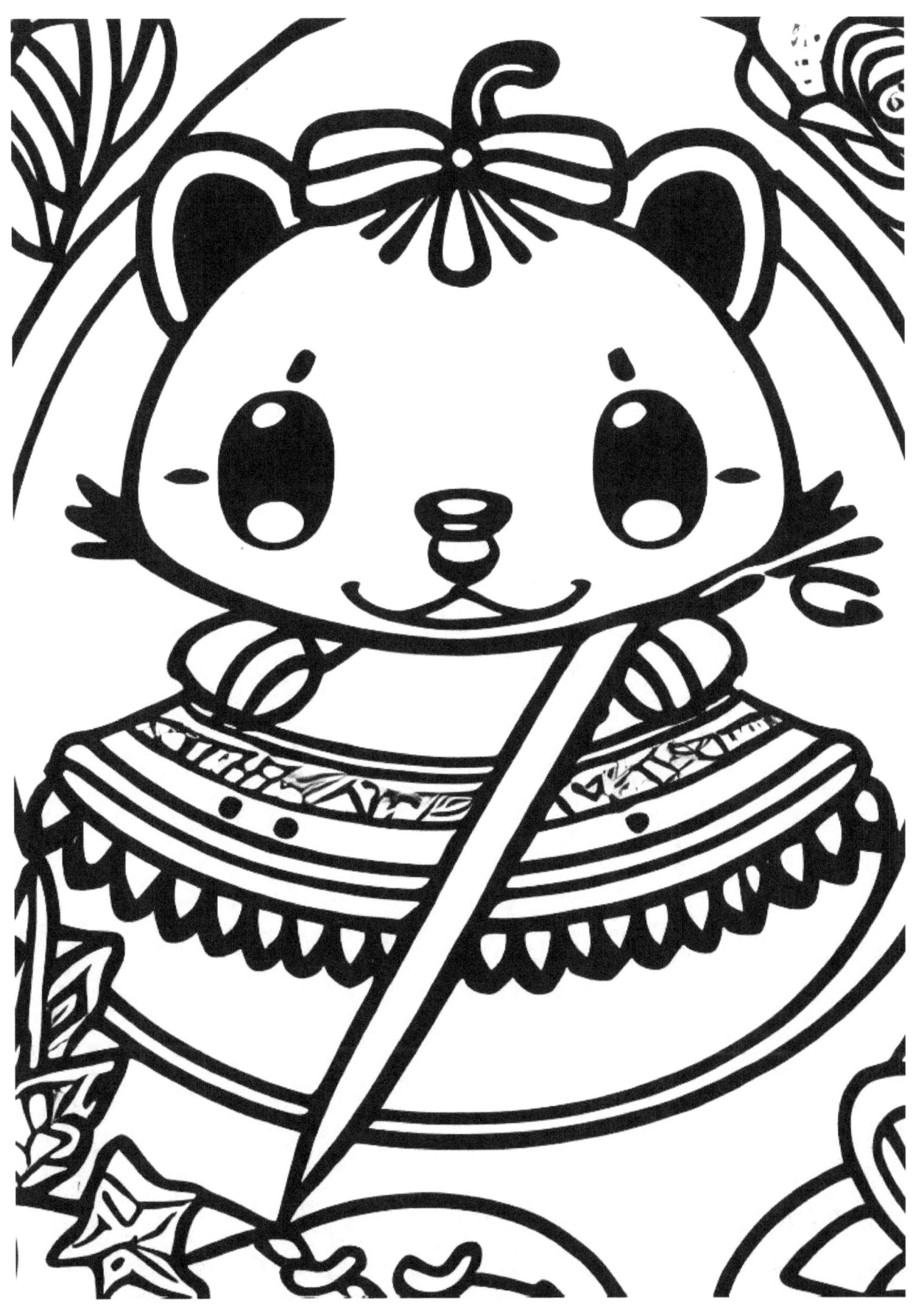

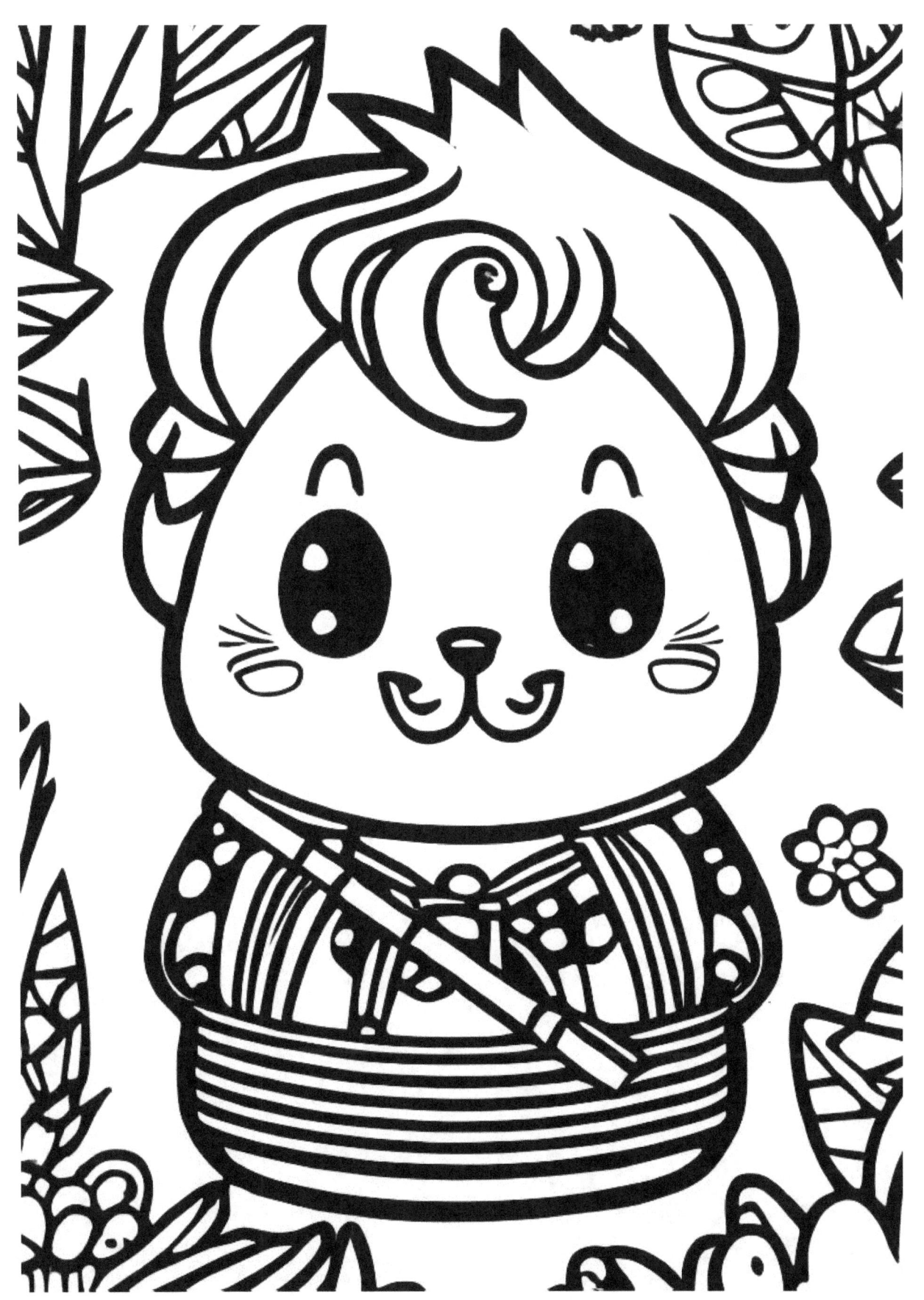

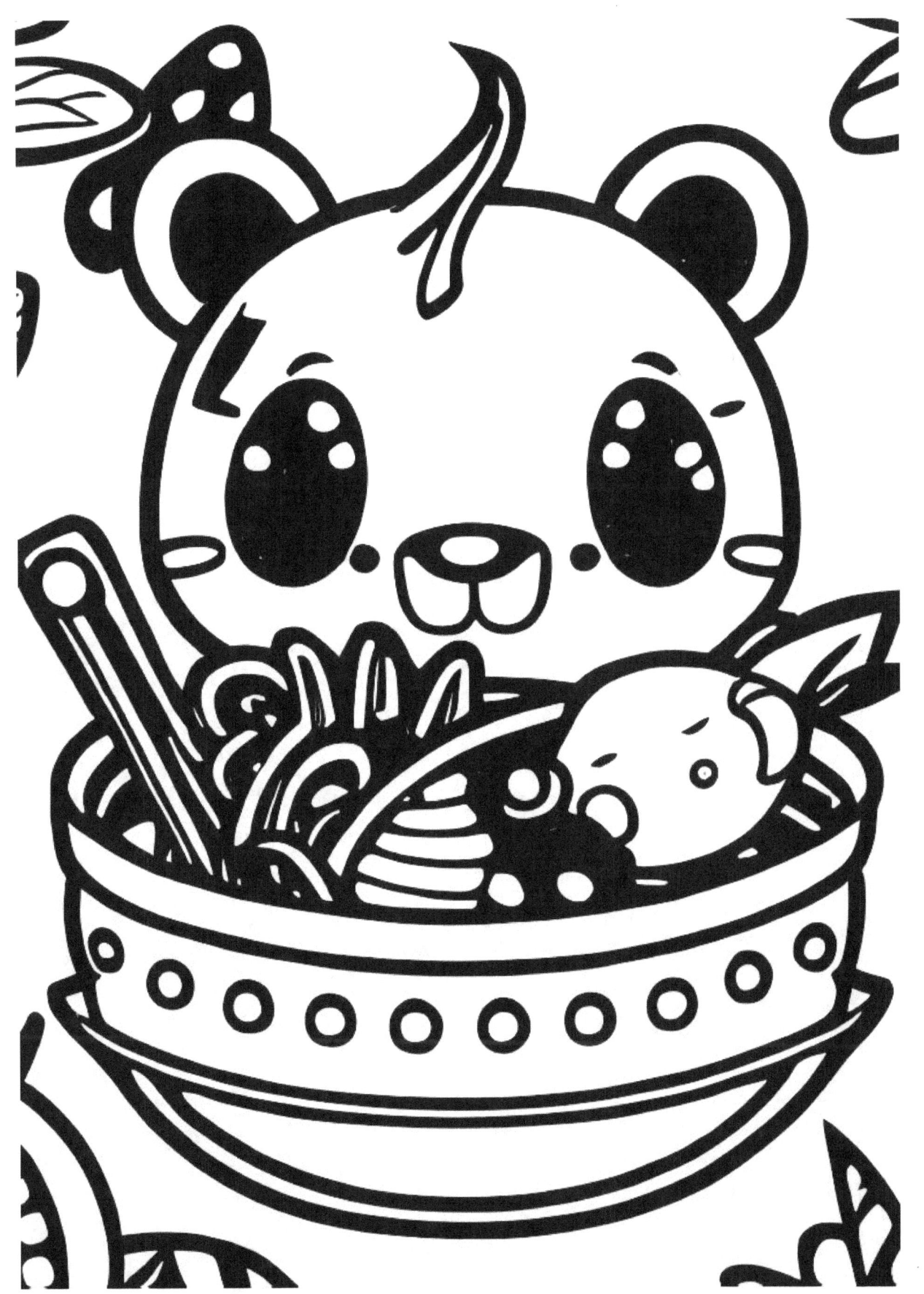

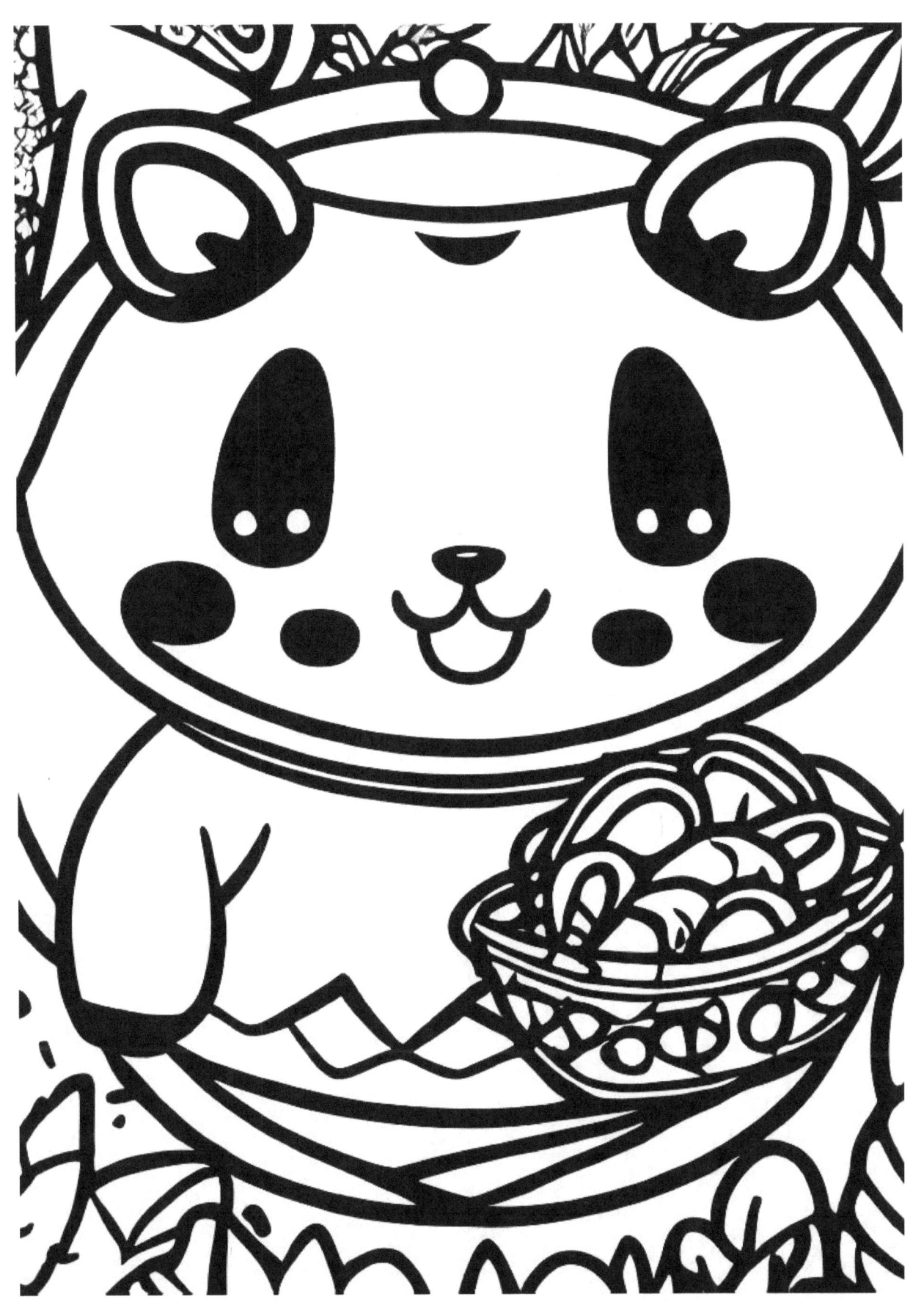

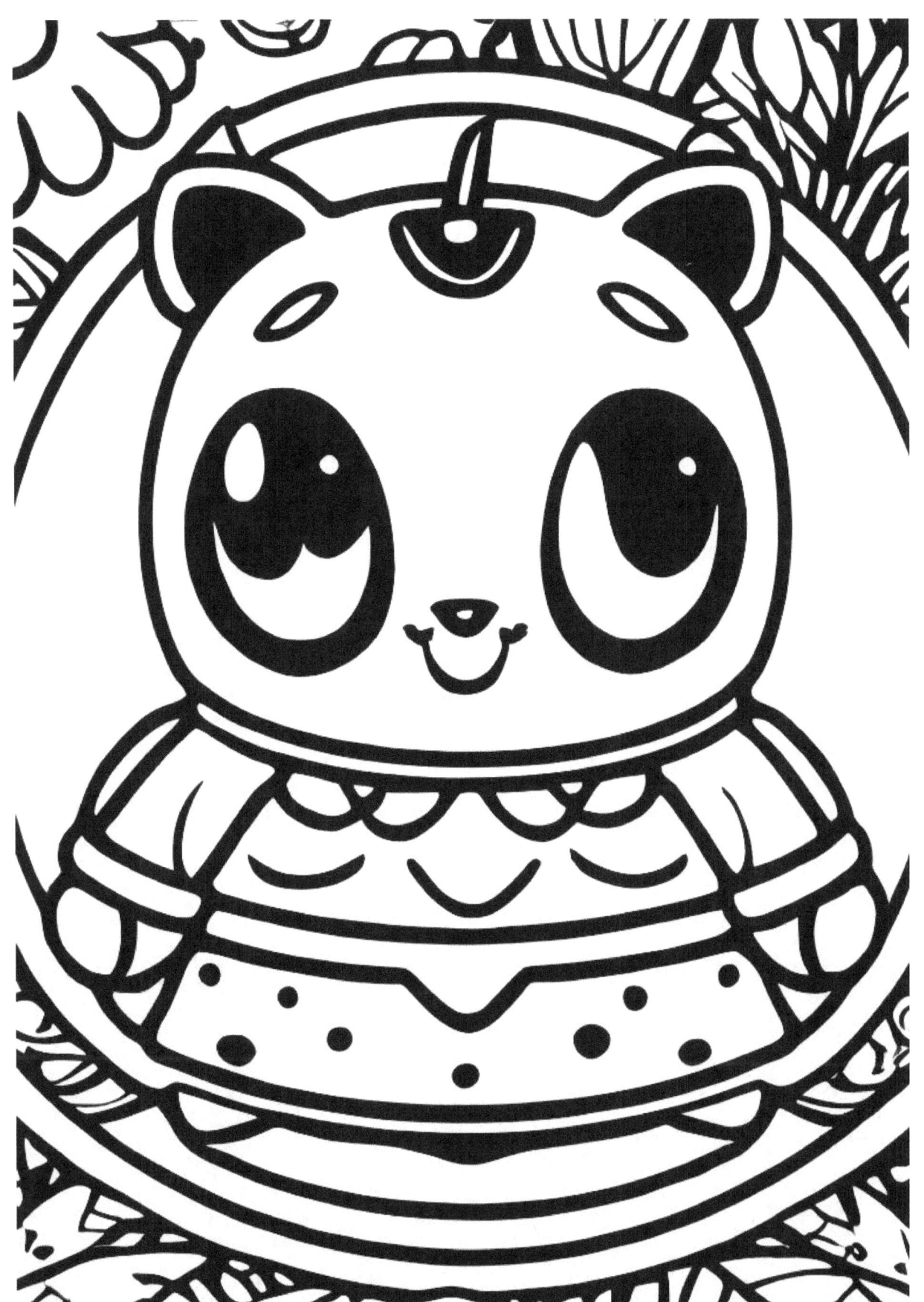

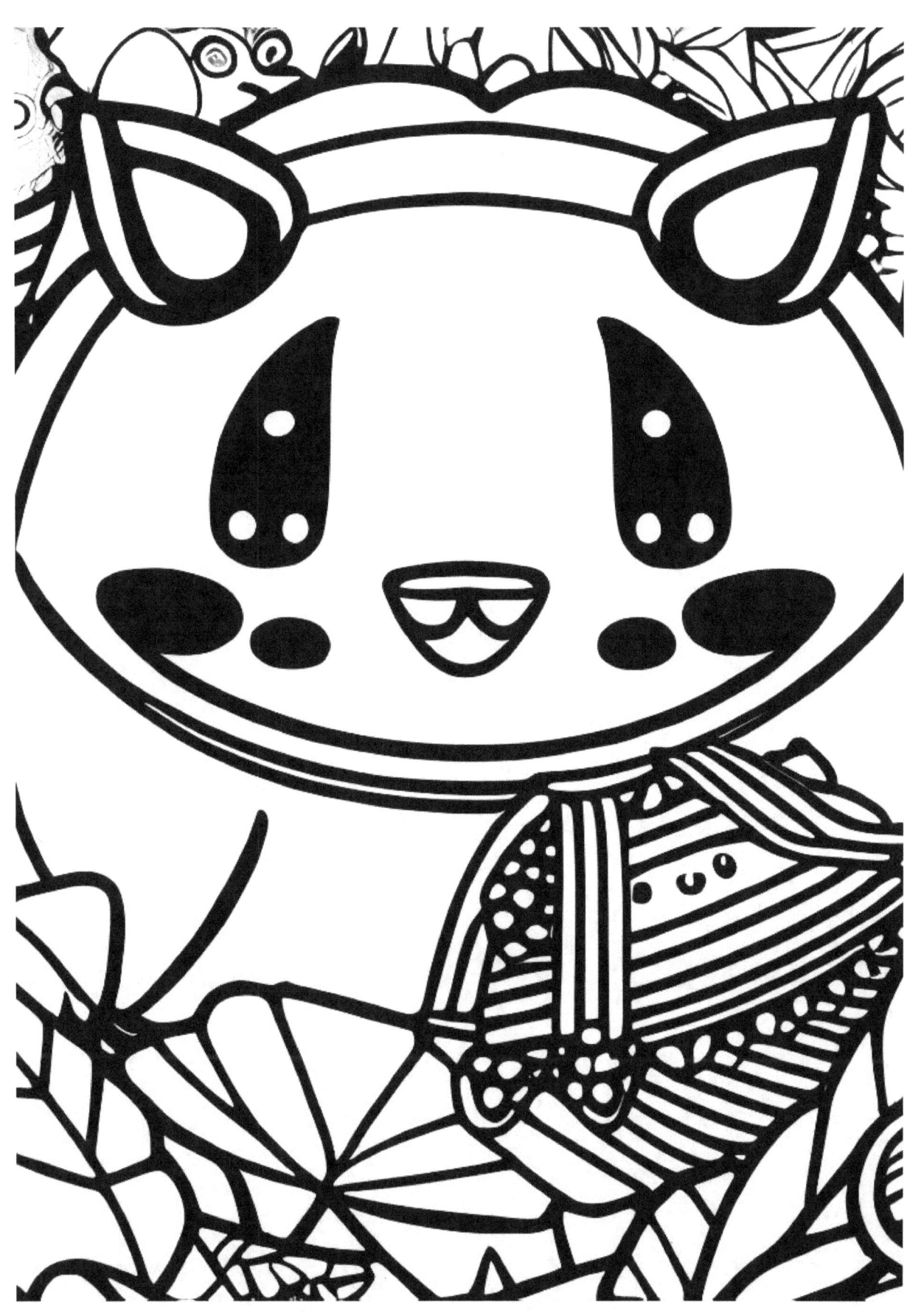

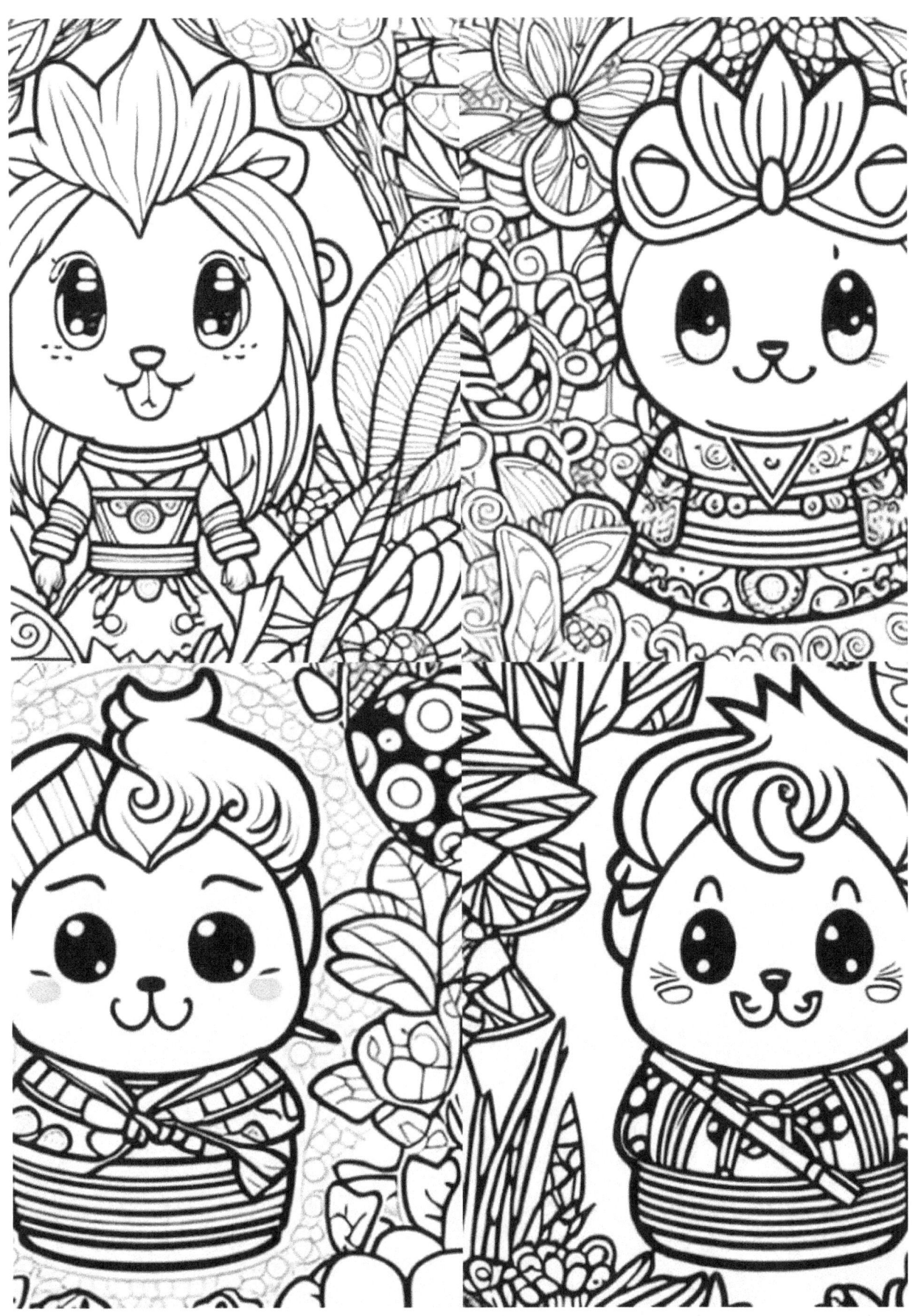

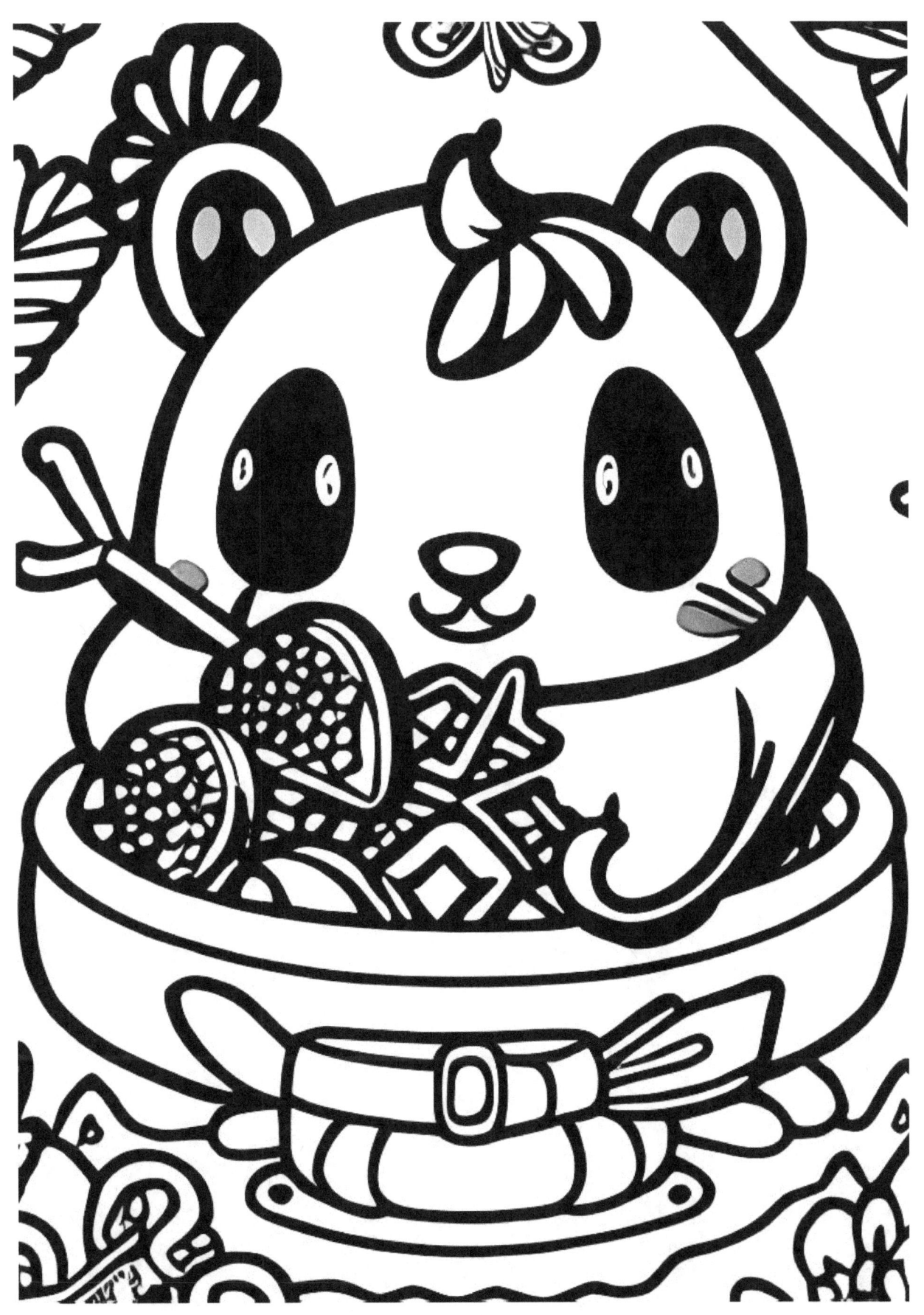

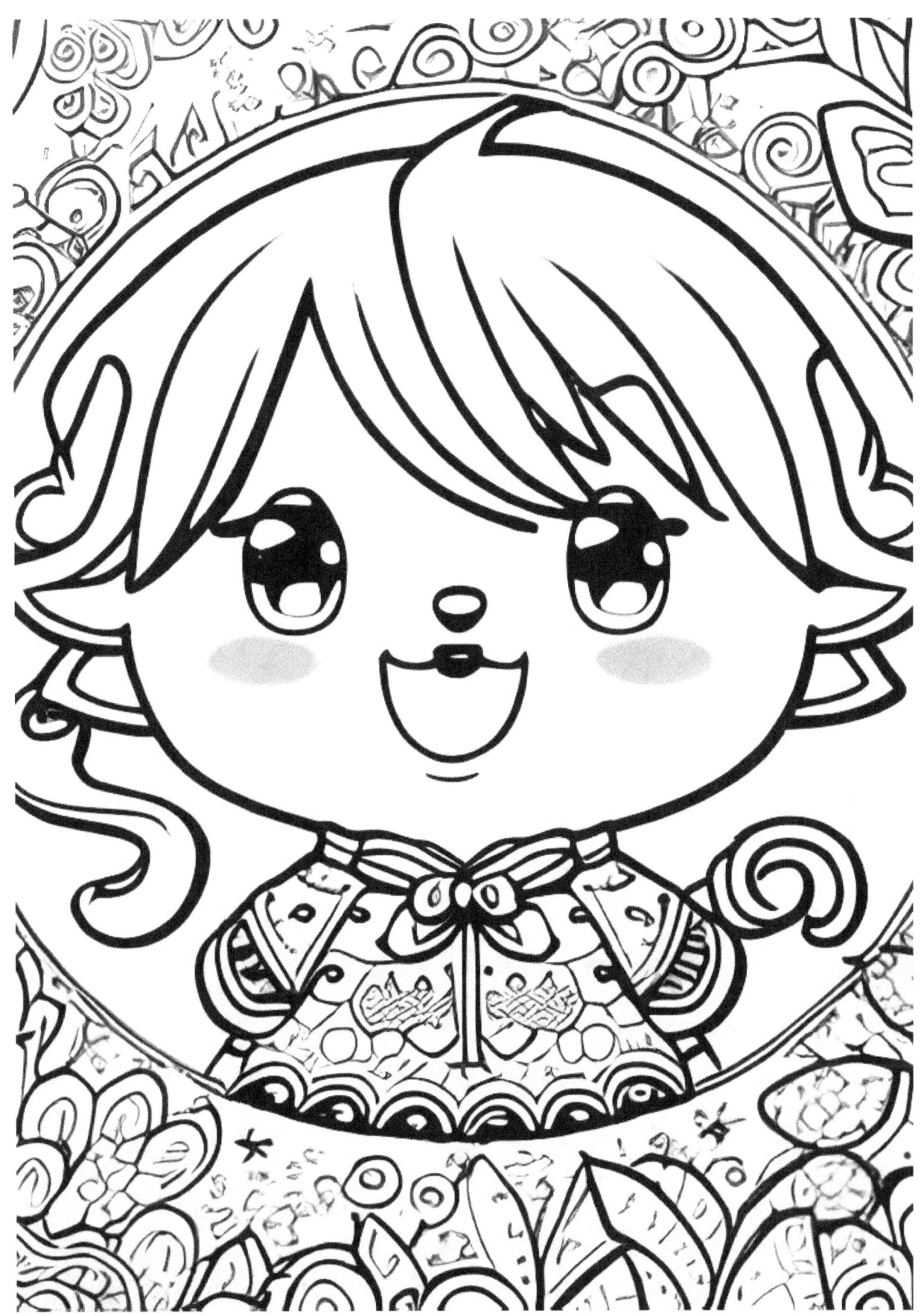

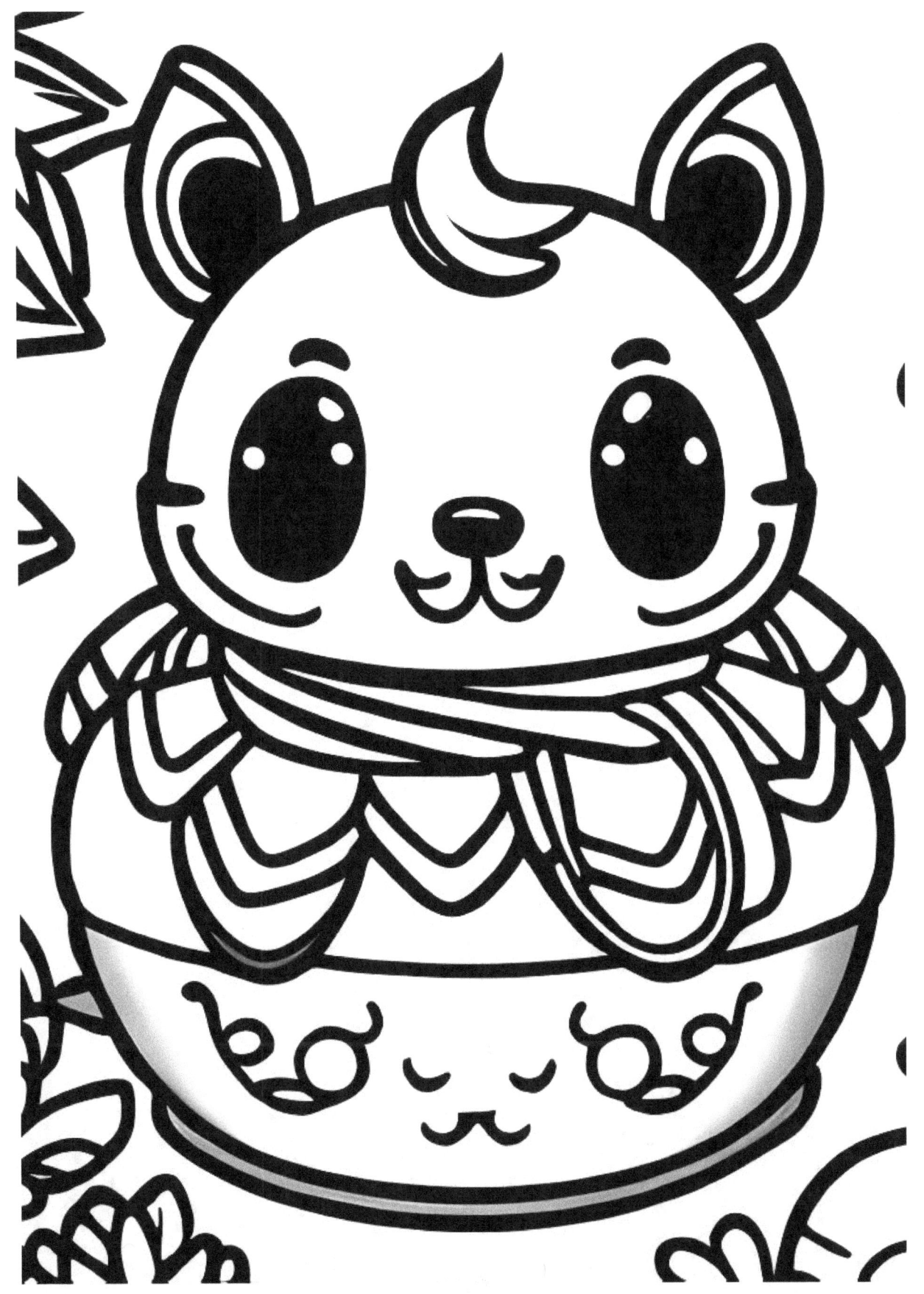

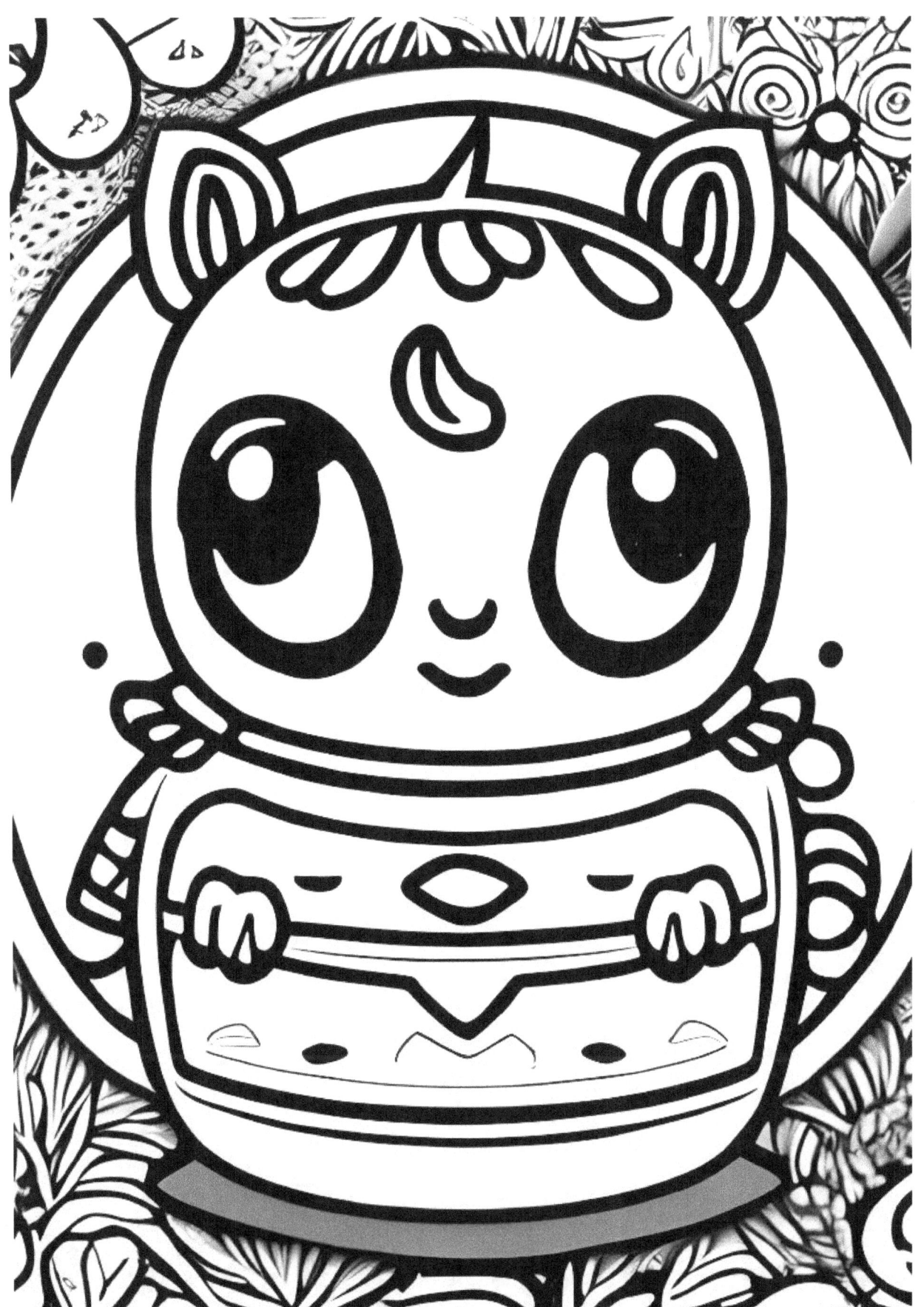

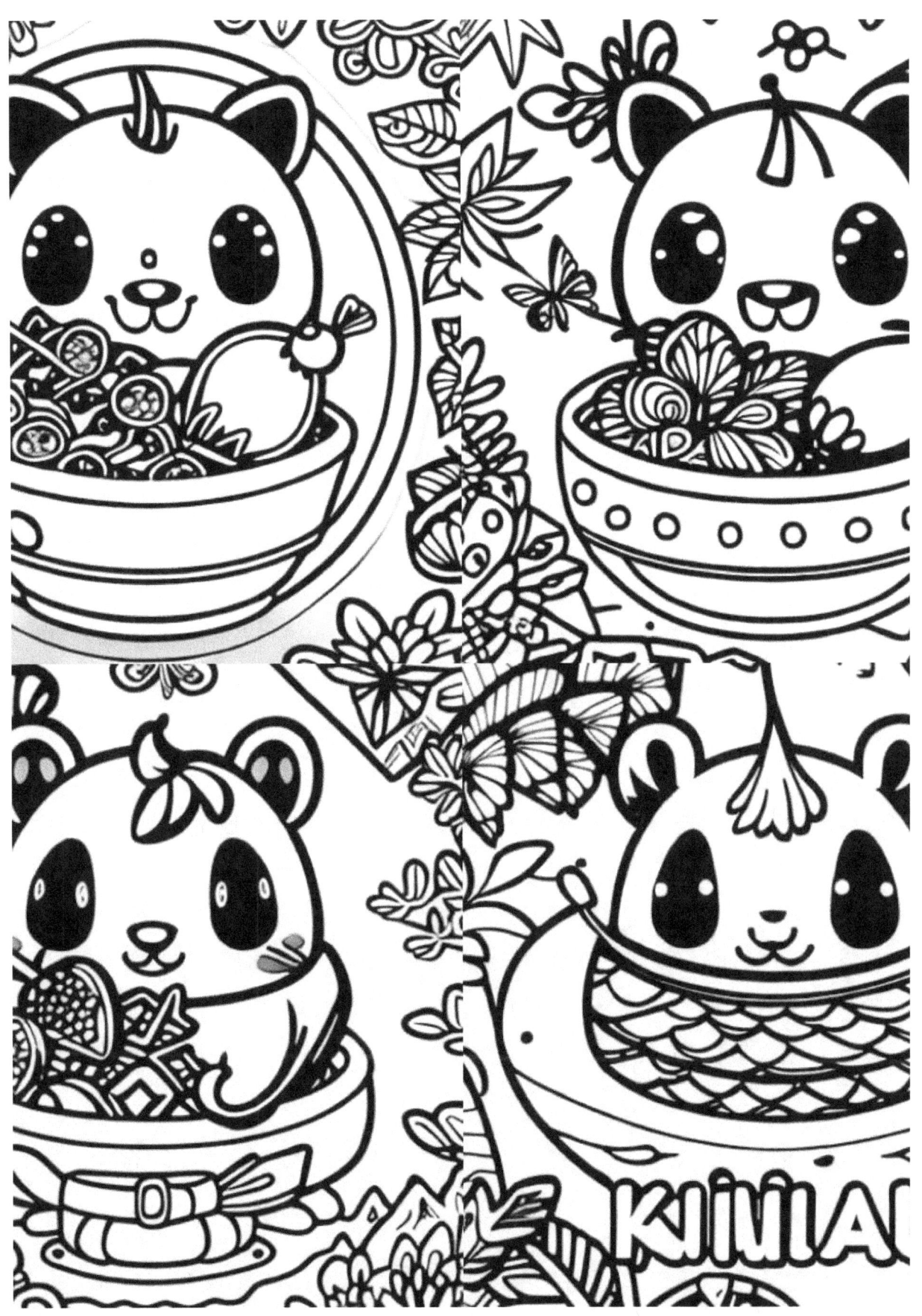

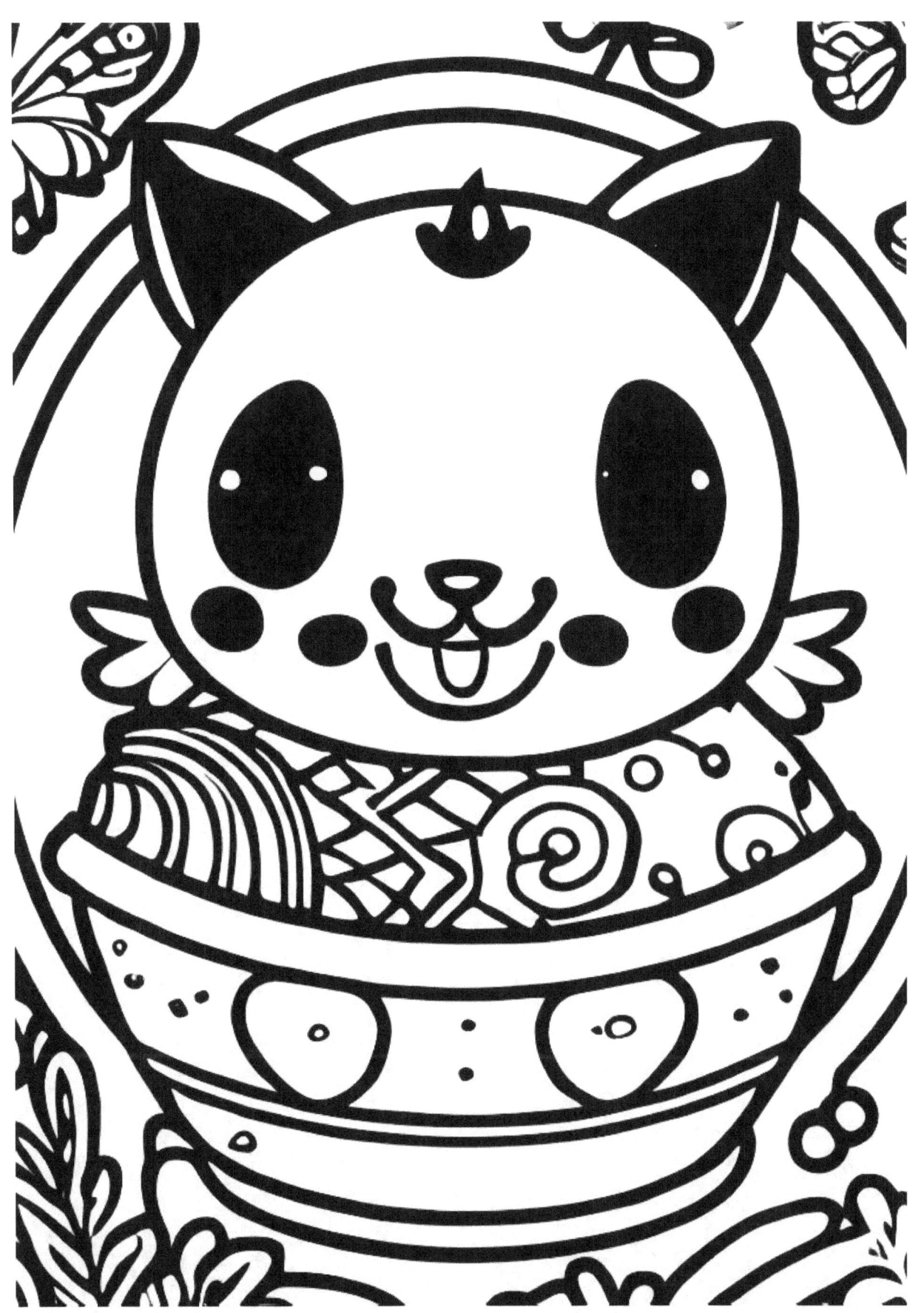

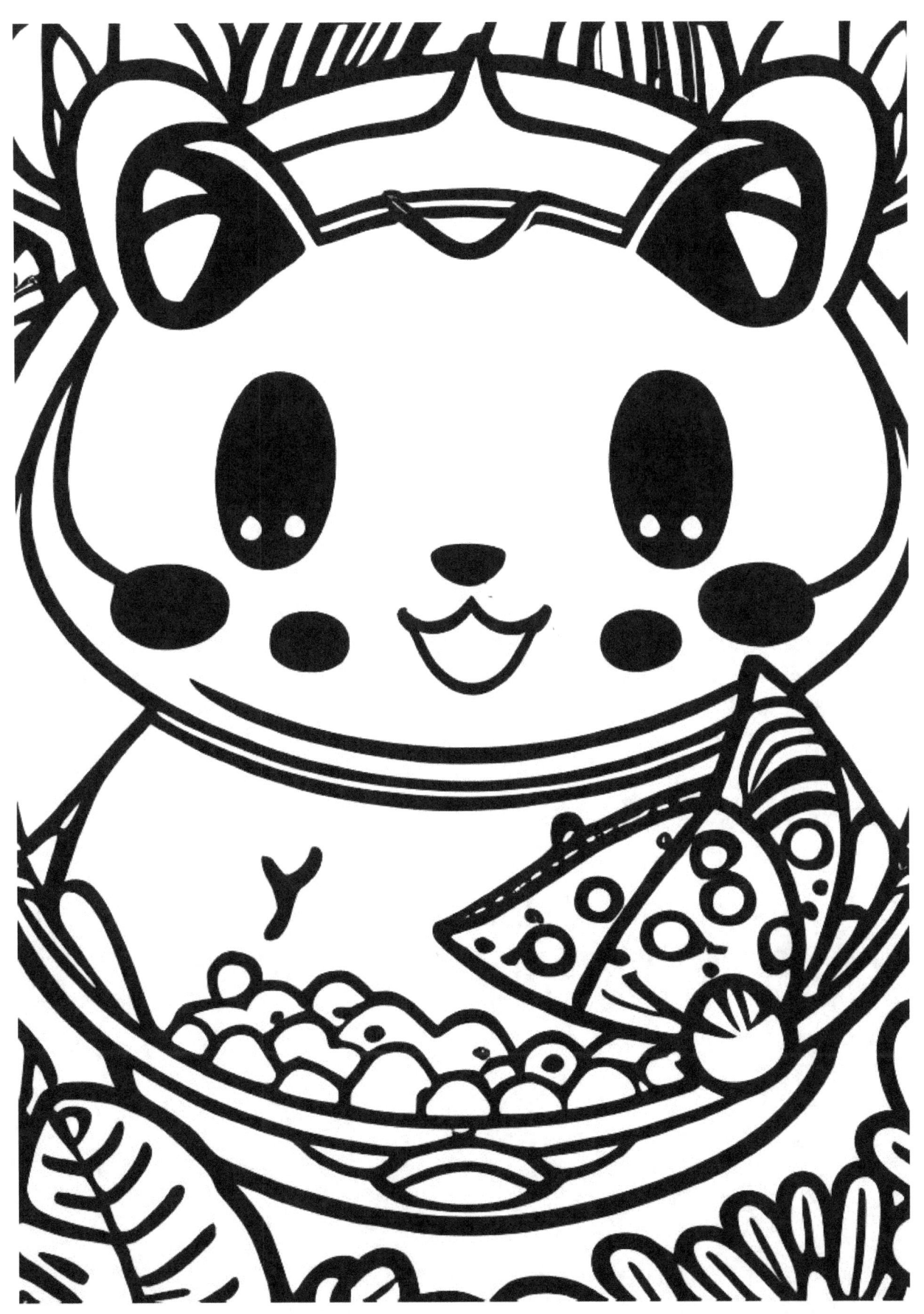

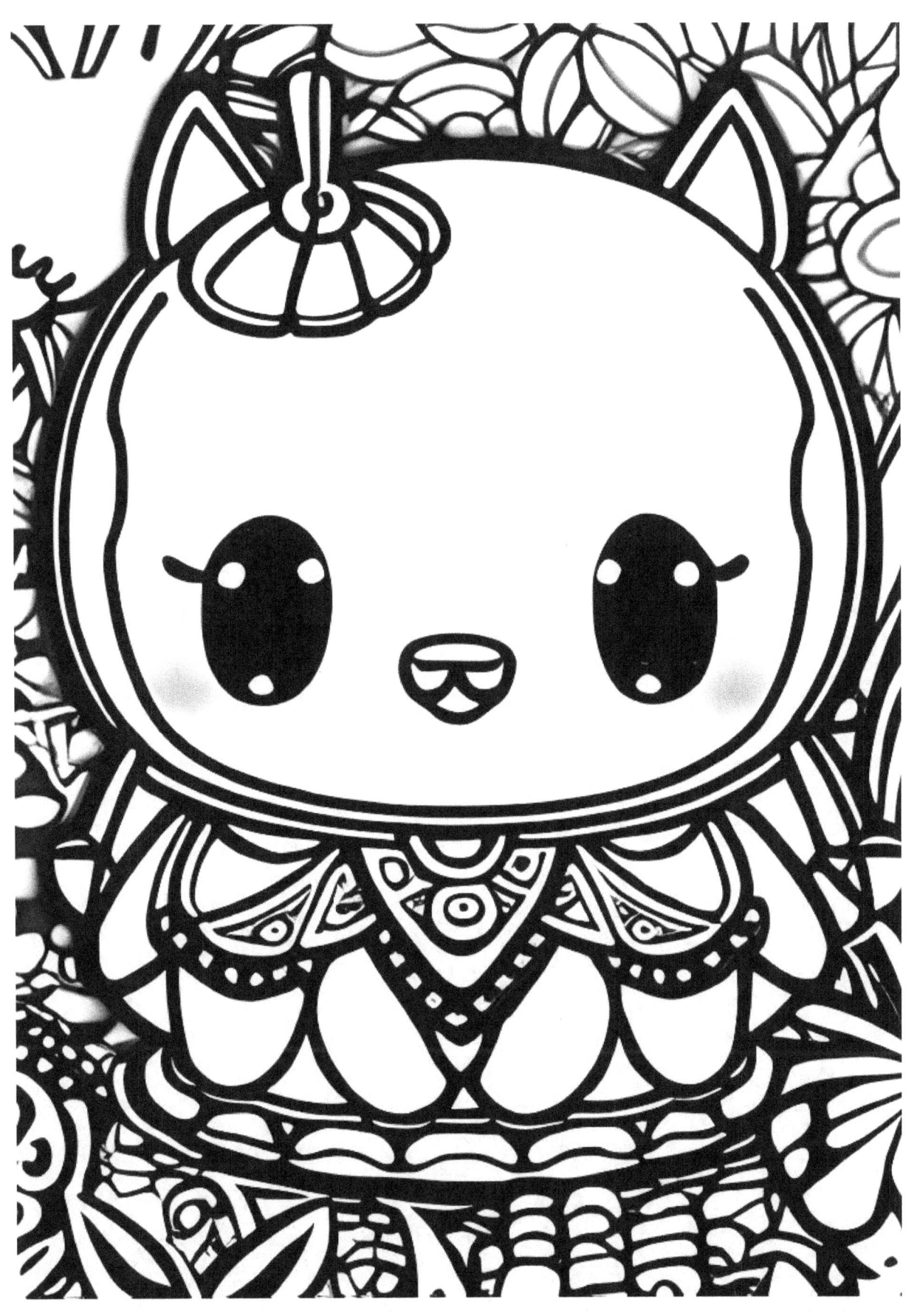

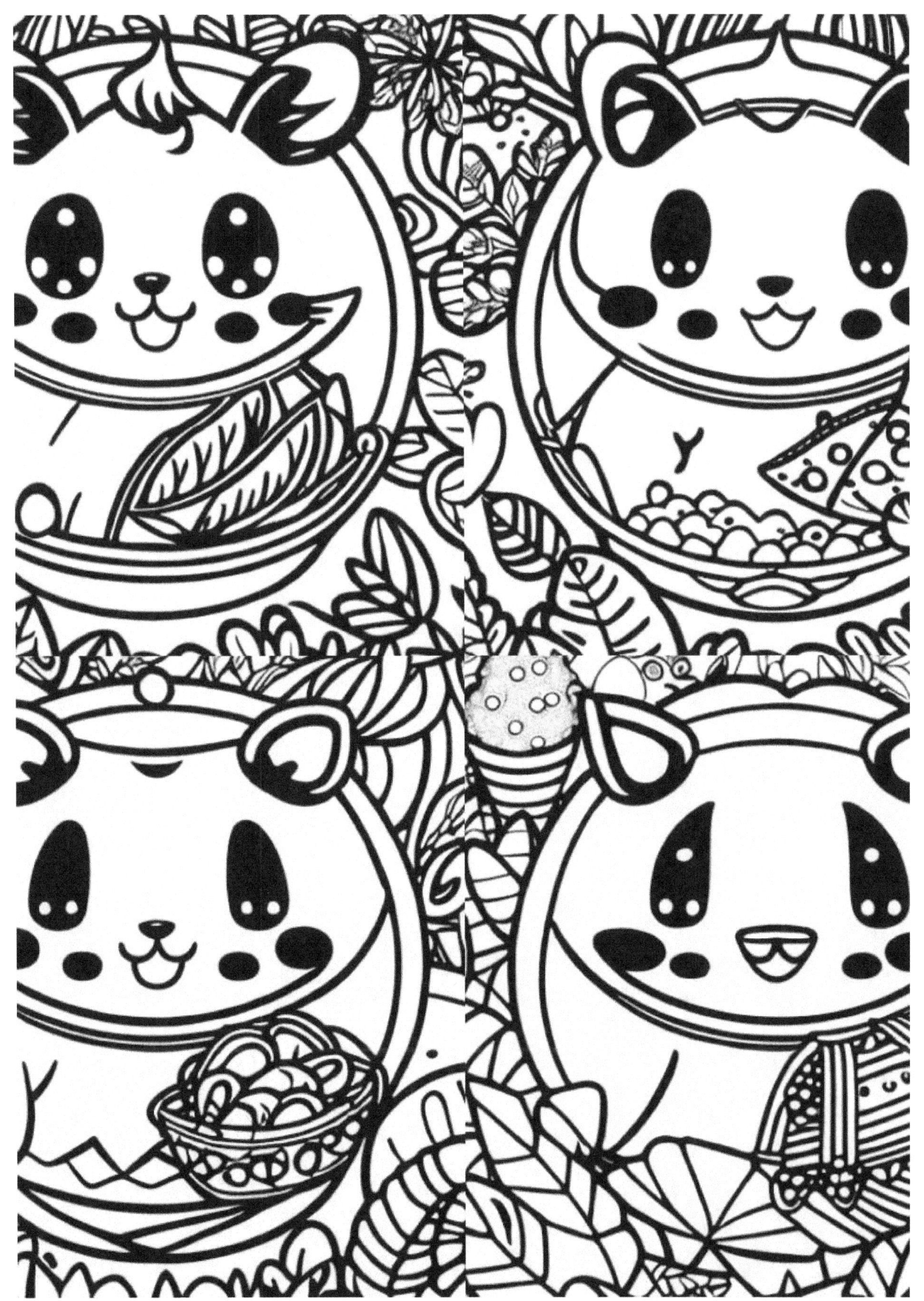

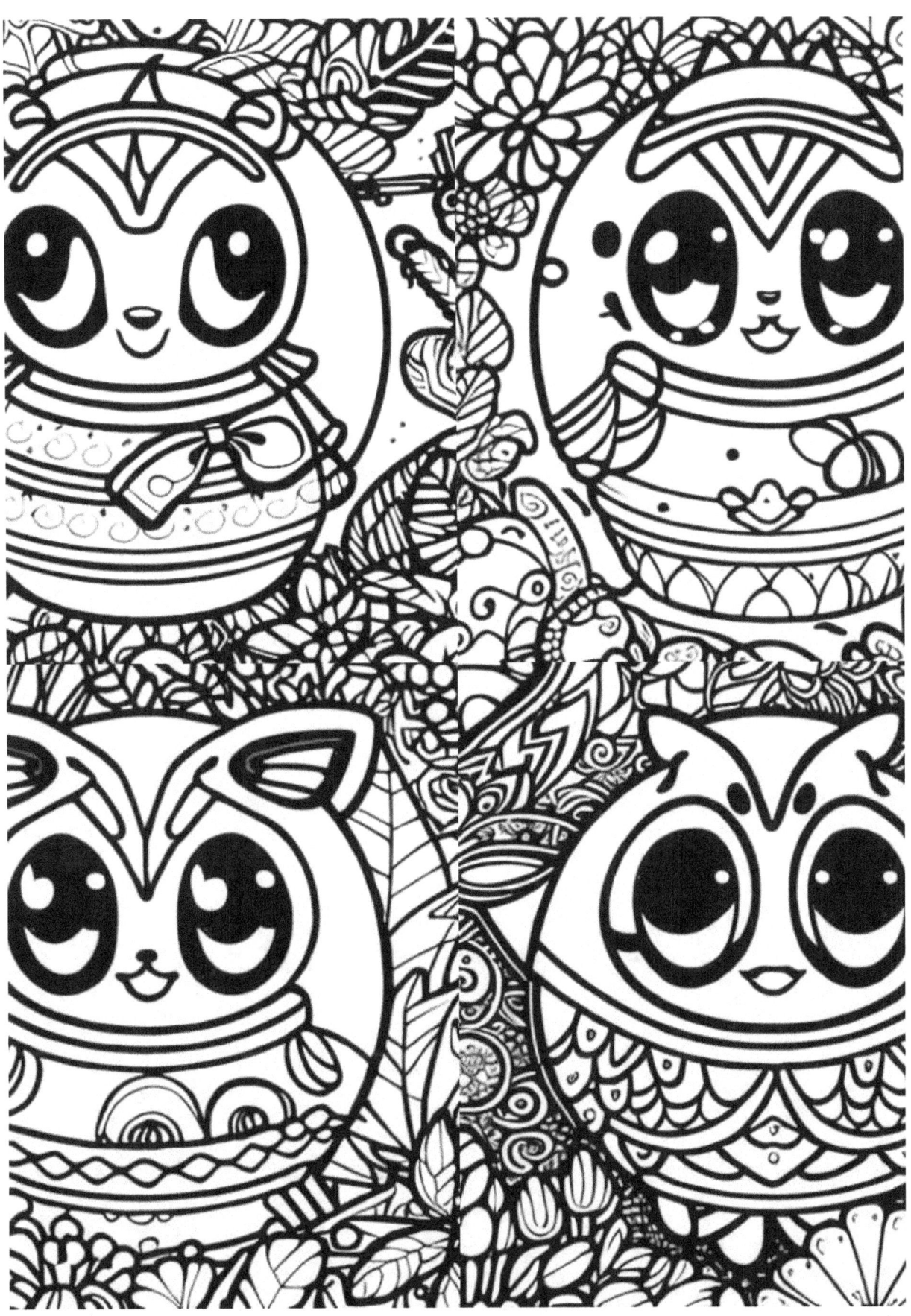

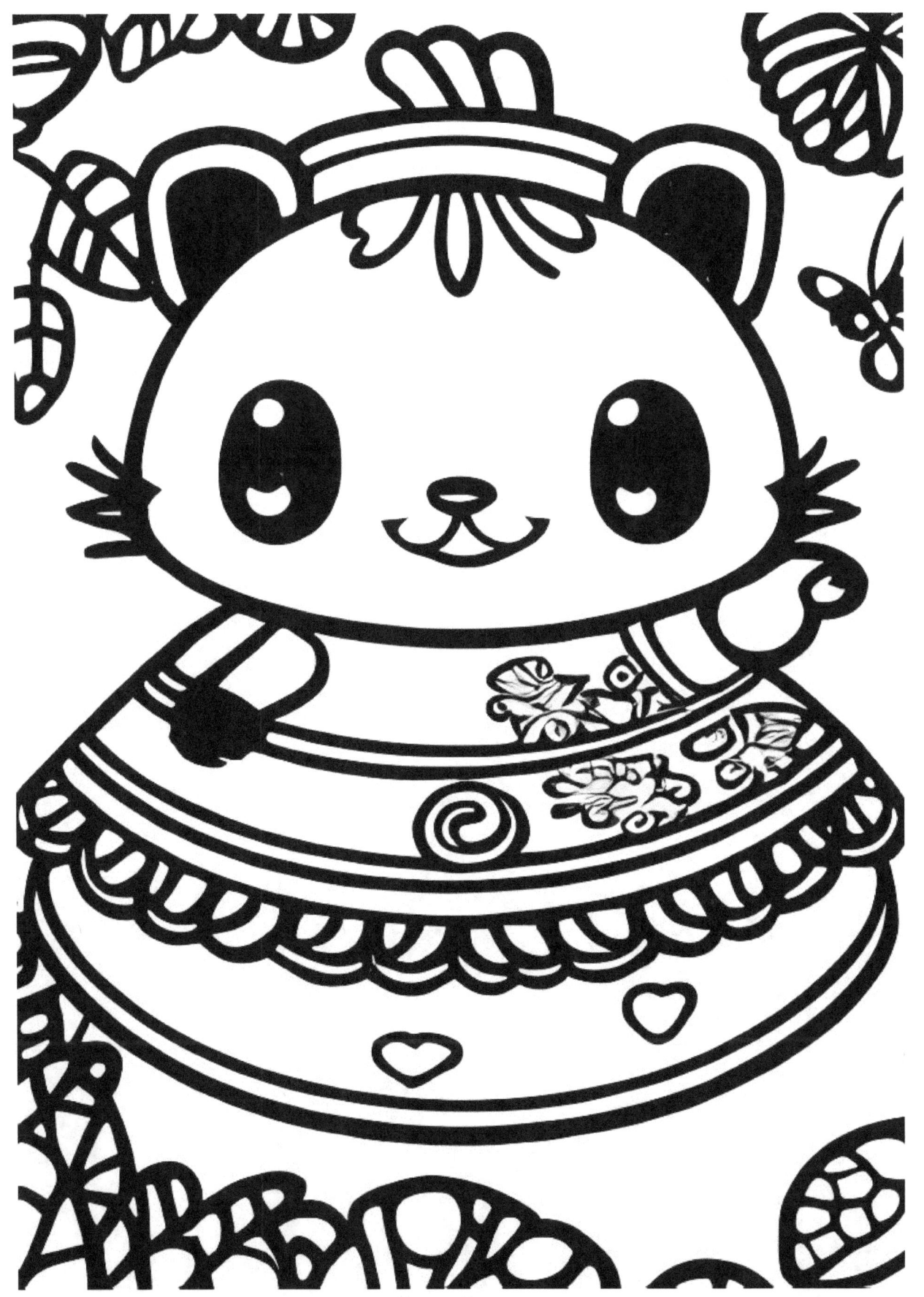

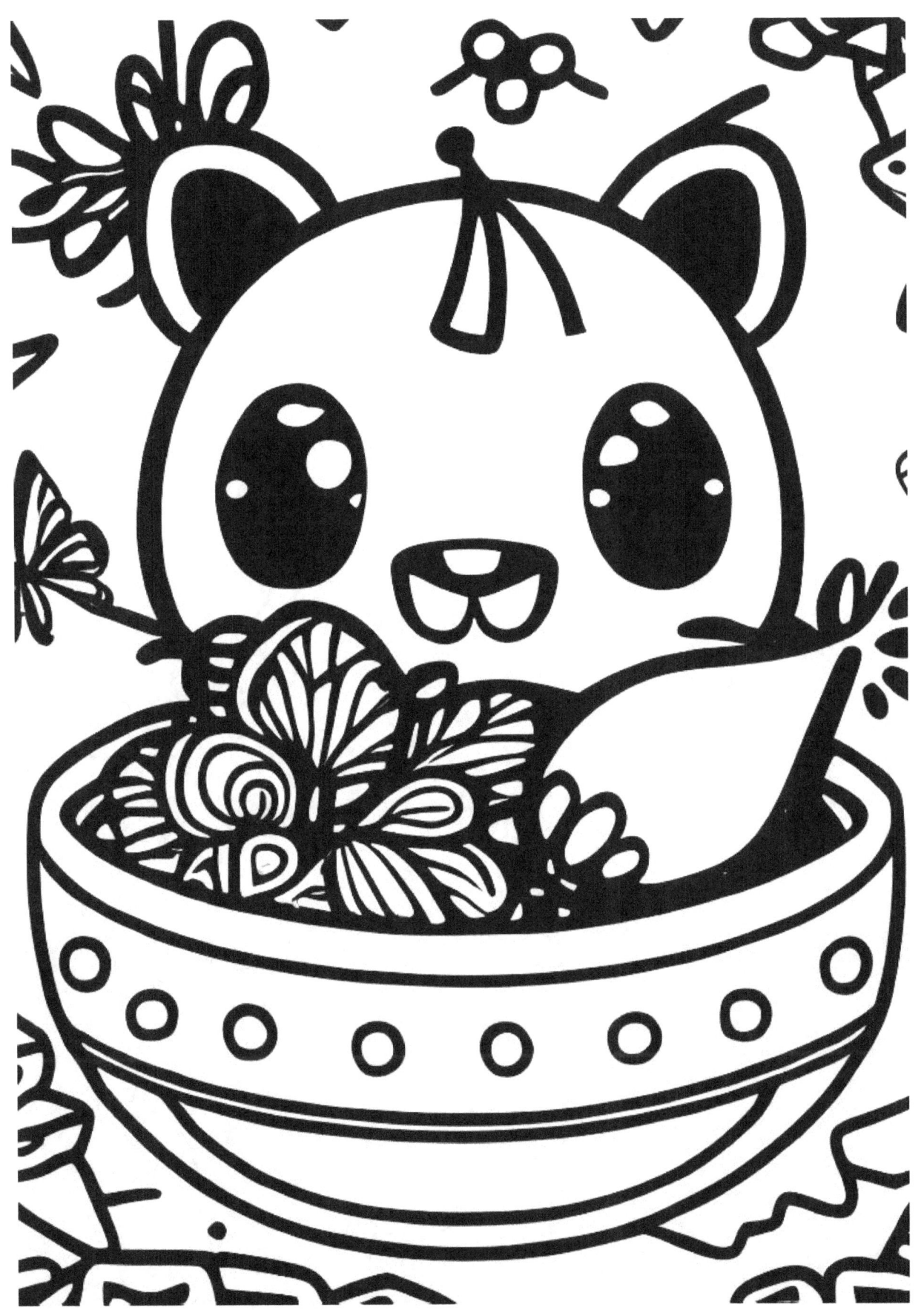

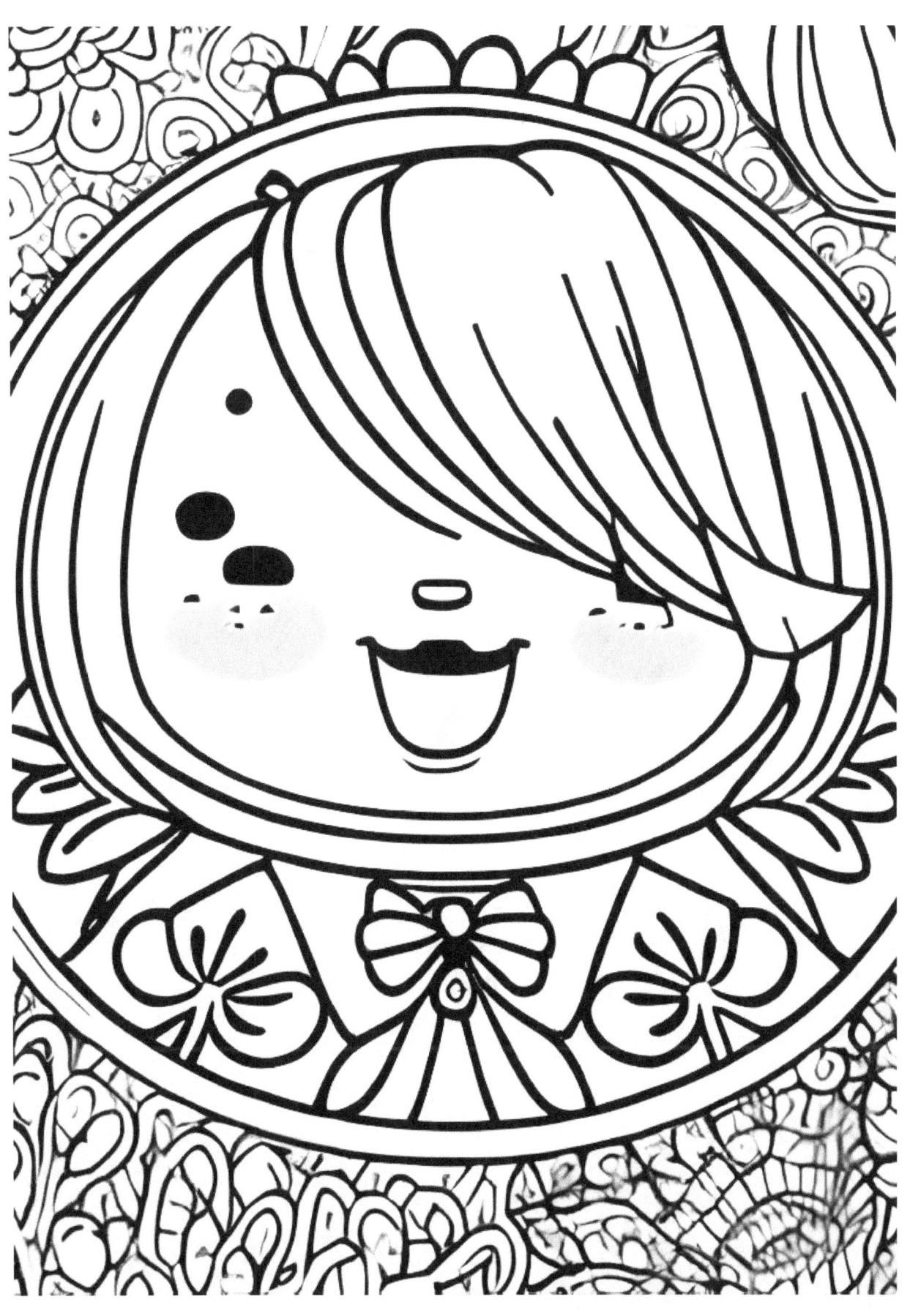

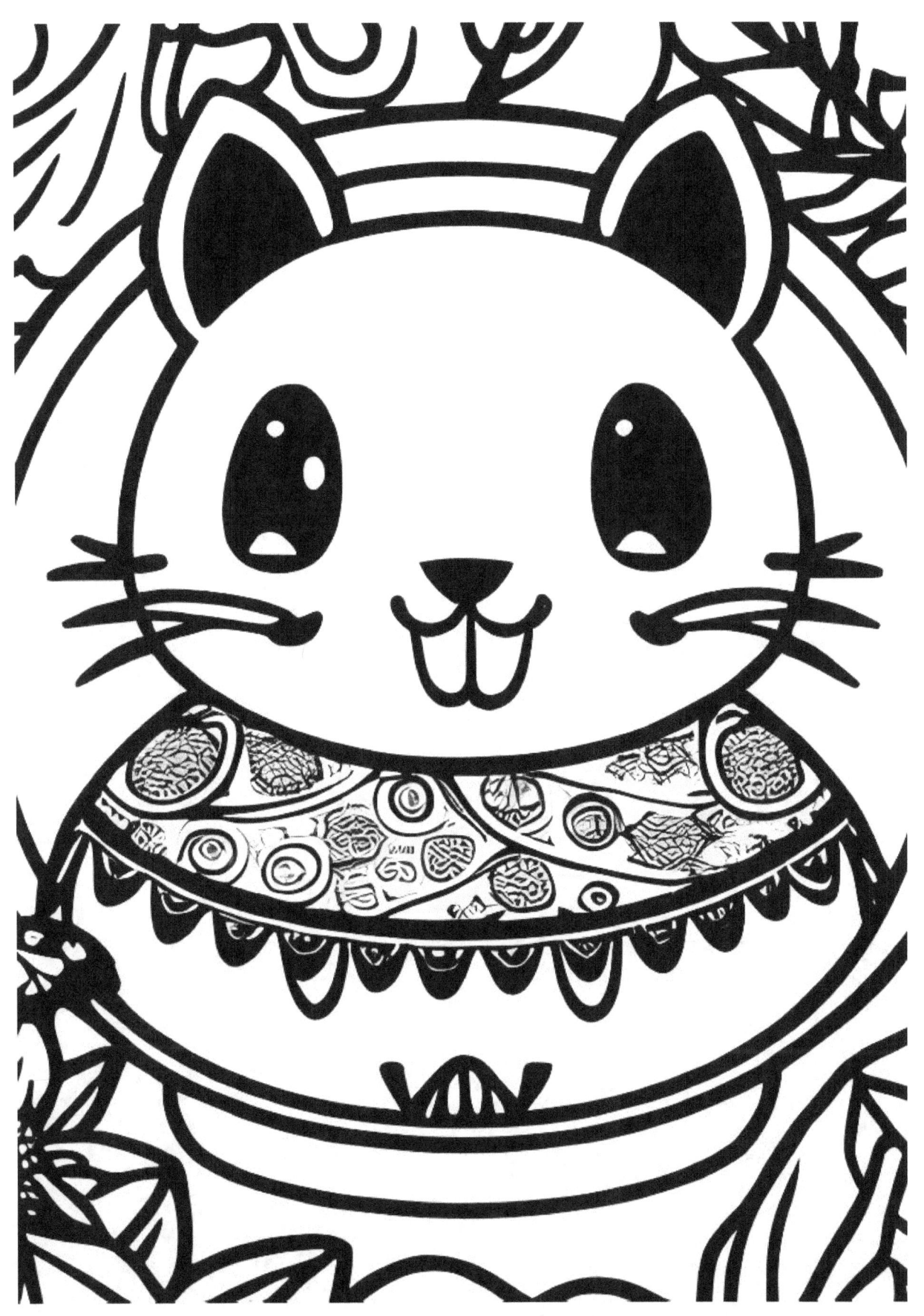

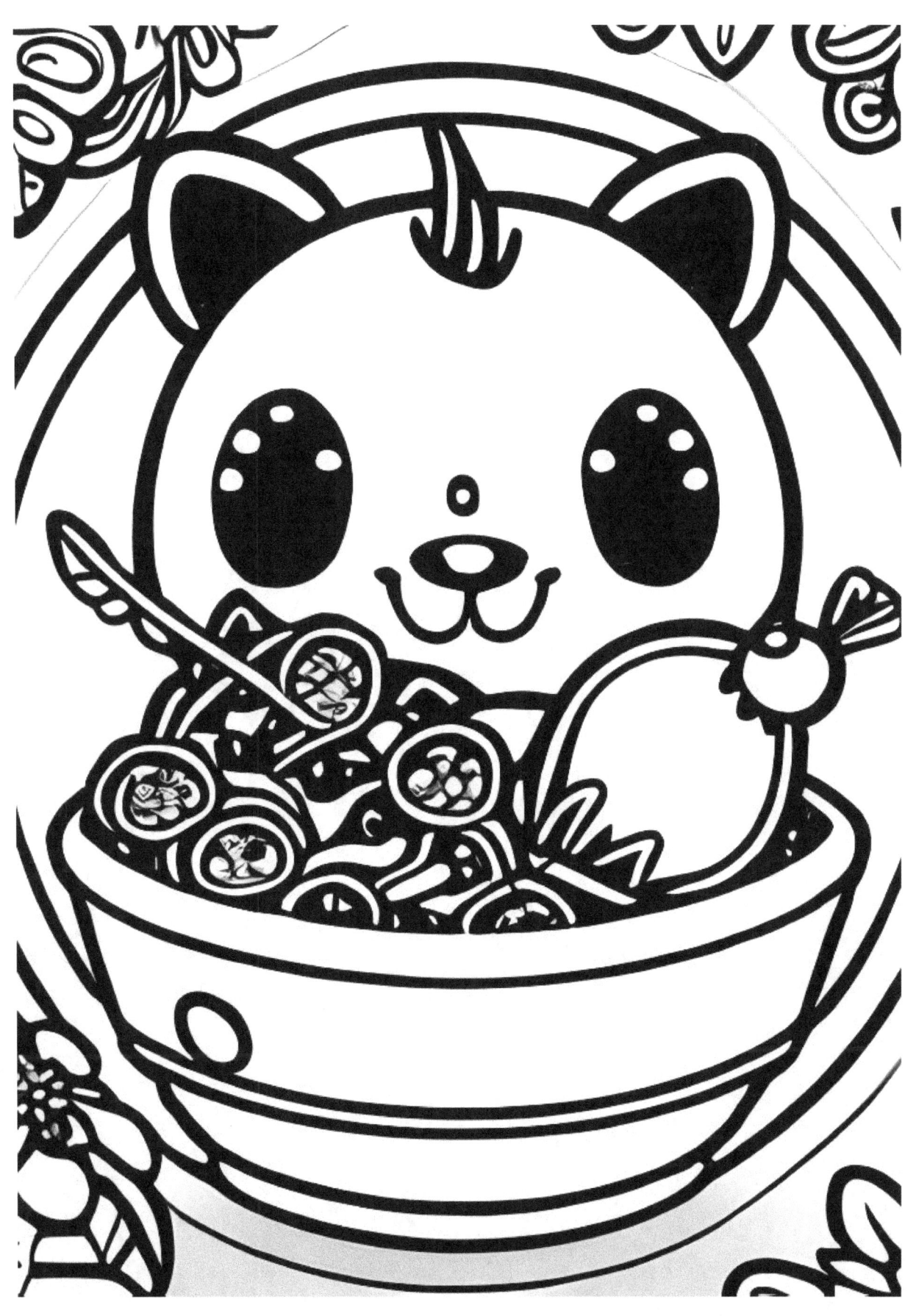

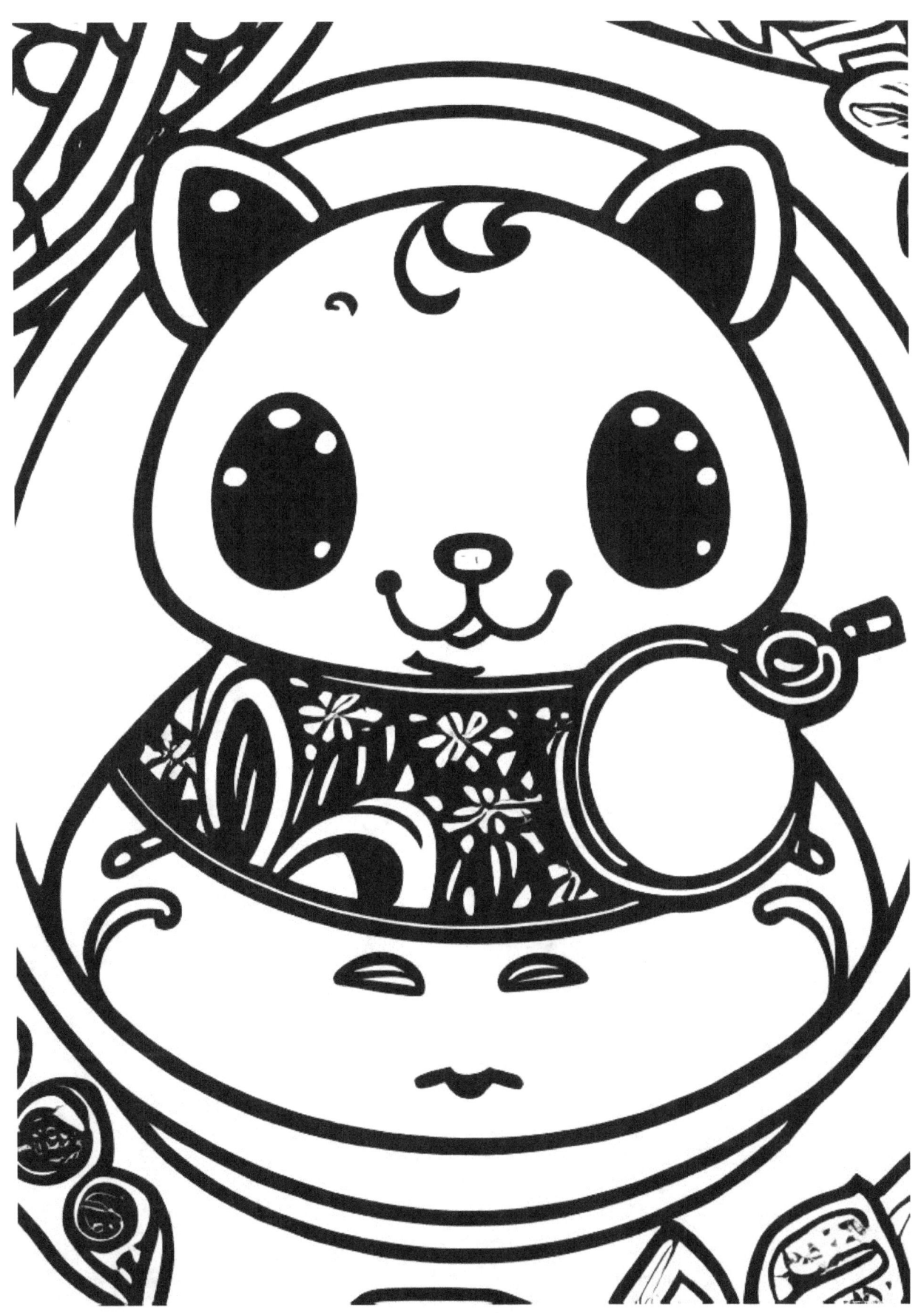

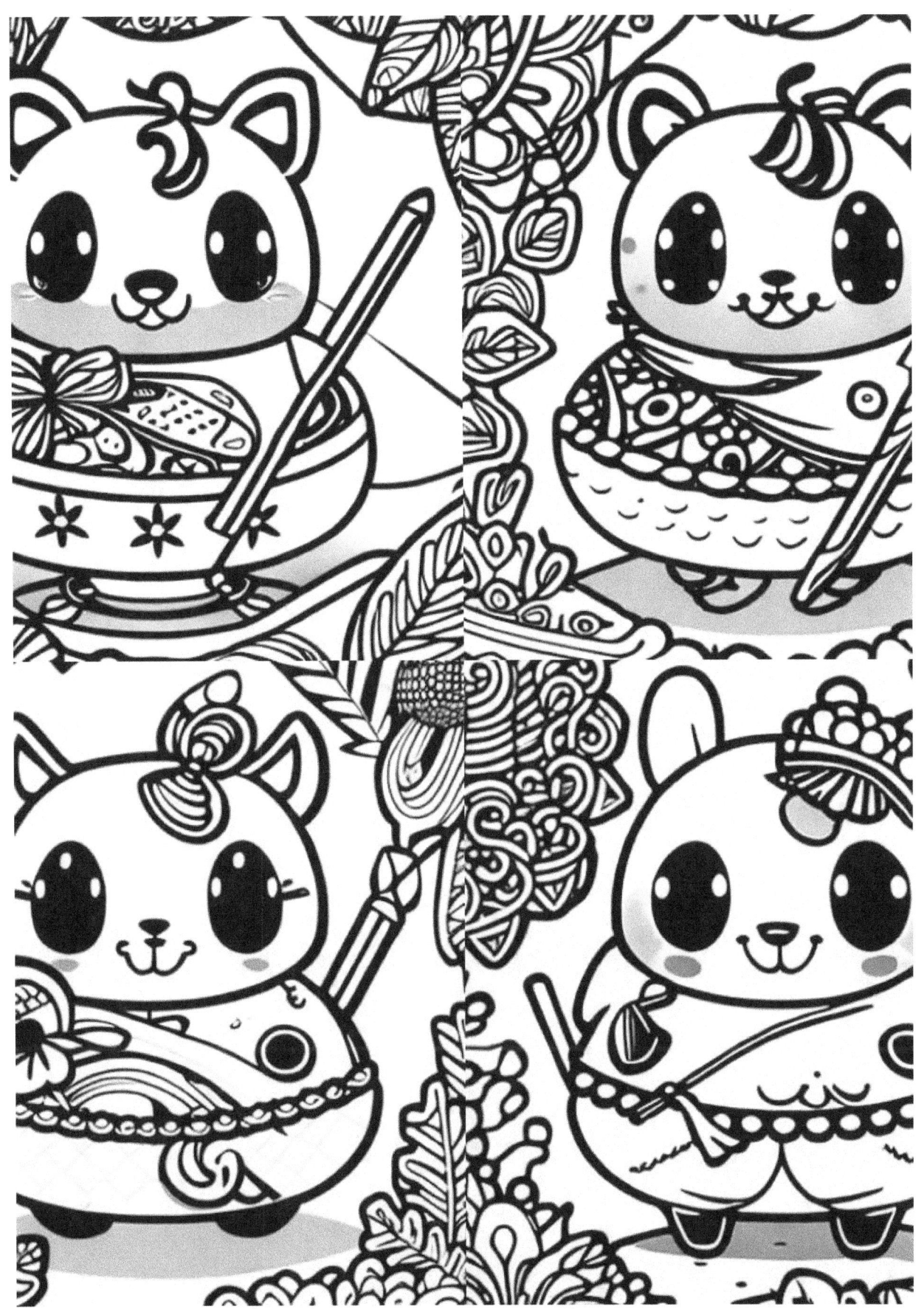

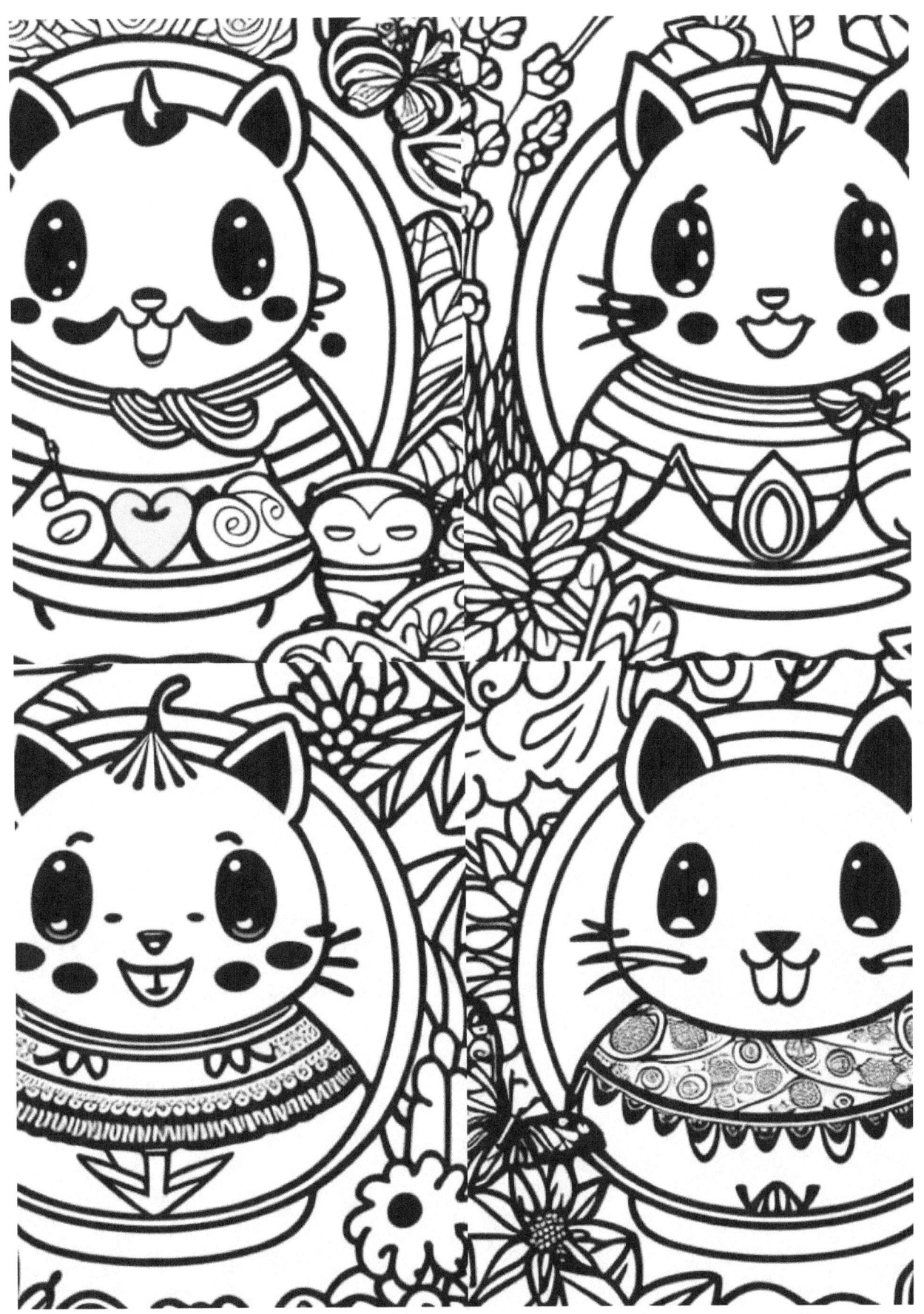